A Scriptural Rosary with Meditations

by
St. Alphonsus de Liguori

Our Lady's Psalter — The Rosary.
There are 150 Hail Marys in the full 15 decades,
corresponding to the number of the Psalms of
David.   Like the Psalms, the Rosary is excel-
lently adapted to prayer in common.

(Pope Leo XIII)

**"THE INCARNATION, BIRTH AND
INFANCY OF JESUS CHRIST"**
&
"THE PASSION AND THE DEATH OF JESUS CHRIST"
by St. Alphonsus de Ligouri
Copyright 1927 By
VERY REV. JAMES BARRON, C.S.s.R.

THE GLORIES OF MARY
by St. Alphonsus de Ligouri
Copyright 1931 By
VERY REV. ANDREW B. KUHN, C.S.s.R.

Reprints from **THE FATIMA CRUSADER**

1) FRONT INSIDE COVER - Sister Lucy Interview
   with Fr. Fuentes, Spring 2005, Issue 79, Pages 20, 22

2) PAGE 88 - July 13th 1917 Apparition.
   Special Introductory Issue, Page 7

3) BACK INSIDE COVER - 15 Promises of the Rosary,
   Winter 2003, Issue 72, Page 35

**Fatima Center website:
www.fatima.org**

The Secret of the Rosary
by St. Louis Marie Grignion de Montfront
Translator: Mary Barbour, T.O.P.
Copyright 1954

THE PRAYER BOOK
Copyright 1954
The Catholic Press, Inc.

Library of Congress Number: TXu 1-768-729
Copyright © August 4, 2011.
All Rights Reserved. Reproduction in any manner is pro-
hibited without written permission from the publisher.

ISBN: 978-0-9839456-0-4

Contents

ART CREDITS:

Gustave Dore from Holy Bible 1914, on page 30.

Swedish Bible 1890, page 70.

Ben Stahl commissioned by the Catholic Press, Inc. in 1954 for the publication THE PRAYER BOOK on pages 32, 60 & 68.

Acquired Copyright for all other artwork from Restored Traditions at *restoredtraditions.com*.

Our Lady's Psalter Publications, LLC
P.O. Box 665, Tavares, FL 32778-0665

WEBSITE: www.OurLadysPsalter.com

Behold, there came wise men from the East, to Jerusalem.

Saying, 'Where is He that is born king of the Jews? For
we have seen His star in the east, and are come to adore Him.'

*

And king Herod hearing this, was troubled,
and all Jerusalem with him

*

Assembling together all the chief priests and the scribes
he inquired of them where Christ should be born.

*

And thou Bethlehem the land of Juda
art not the least among the princes of Juda:

*

for out of thee shall come forth the captain
that shall rule My people Israel.

*

Herod sending them into Bethlehem said,
'When you have found Him, bring me word again,
that I also may come and adore Him.'

*

Behold the star which they had seen in the east,
went before them, until it came and
stood over where the Child was.

*

And entering into the house,
they found the Child with Mary His Mother,

*

and falling down they adored Him; they offered Him
gifts: gold, frankincense, and myrrh.

Matt 2:1-11

Why Pray This Rosary

The Dominicans have an ancient tradition that the Rosary was given to Saint Dominic by Our Lady while he was combating the Albigensian heresy in the south of France, early in the thirteenth century. Others believe that the Rosary was in use long before Saint Dominic's time, in the form of Our Lady's Psalter, a series of 150 Aves said as a kind of substitute for the 150 Psalms of the Psalter. Regardless of its origins, the Rosary has proved an astonishingly effective implement of Christian piety and, as Pope Leo XIII declared, the best and most fruitful means of invoking Our Lady. Mary Herself has expressed Her predilection for this prayer, notably in Her appearances at Lourdes, France in 1858 and also at Fatima, Portugal in 1917. She prayed this form of the Psalter (rosary) with Bernadette at Lourdes and with the three shepherd children at Fatima. Mary requested it to be said everyday, at all of the apparitions.

This booklet contains two forms of devotion of the Rosary. The main prayers are the 54 day Novena. It consists of 27 days in petition and 27 days in thanksgiving and is explained in greater detail on page 10.

It also contains a form of Scriptural prayers. Each of the decades has a designated line of scripture for each Hail Mary. You are not obligated to strictly follow this method. You can also just use one or two of the scriptures for that decade to meditate on. Also you can say the prayers for the mysteries (in Petition) and then turn to the corresponding mystery (in Thanksgiving) and use those prayers for the decades. The prayers for the decades are identical. The prayers for the mysteries at the beginning of the set of mysteries is different from petition and thanksgiving. Also included is an extra set of scripture for the Nativity dealing with the 3 Kings on page 4 and for the Resurrection dealing with doubting Thomas on page 87.

Our Lady also taught Blessed Alan de la Roche and said to him in a vision: "When people say one hundred and fifty Hail Mary's this prayer is very helpful to them and is a very pleasing tribute to Me. But they will do better still and will please Me even more if they say these Hail Mary's while meditating on the Life, Death and Passion of Jesus Christ — for this meditation is the soul of this prayer."

ROSARY PRAYERS

THE SIGN OF THE CROSS

Catholics usually begin and end their prayers with the Sign of the Cross. The words of this prayer express faith in the mystery of the Trinity, Father, Son and Holy Ghost; the cross made with the hand while saying the words expresses belief in the redemption accomplished by Christ on the Cross.

The Sign of the Cross *is correctly made by touching, with the joined fingers of the right hand, the forehead while saying* **In the name of the Father**, *the breast while saying* **and of the Son,** *the left, then the right shoulder while saying* **and of the Holy Ghost. Amen.**

In the name of the Father, and of the Son, and of the Holy Ghost. Amen. *Indulgence of 3 years; when made with holy water, 7 years.*

THE APOSTLES' CREED

This profession of faith summarizes the teaching of the Apostles. According to a legend, each of the Apostles contributed one of its twelve articles. But the present form of the Creed seems to go back to about the third century.

I believe in God, the Father Almighty, Creator of Heaven and earth; and in Jesus Christ, His only Son, Our Lord; who was conceived by the Holy Ghost, born of the Virgin Mary, suffered under Pontius Pilate, was crucified, died, and was buried. He descended into hell; the third day He arose again from the dead; He ascended into Heaven, sitteth at the right hand of God, the Father Almighty; from thence He shall come to judge the living and the dead. I believe in the Holy Ghost, the Holy Catholic Church, the Communion of Saints, the forgiveness of sins, the resurrection of the body, and life everlasting. Amen.

FATIMA PRAYER

Prayer given to the shepherd children by the Blessed Mother to be said at the end of each decade.

O my Jesus, forgive us, save us from the fire of hell. Lead all souls to Heaven, especially those who are most in need.

THE OUR FATHER

This is the prayer taught by Christ Himself (Matt. 6:9-13). The Our Father contains seven petitions, three of them concerned with God's glory, four with man's needs.

Our Father who art in Heaven, hallowed be Thy name; Thy Kingdom come; Thy will be done on earth as it is in Heaven. Give us this day our daily bread; and forgive us our trespasses as we forgive those who trespass against us; and lead us not into temptation, but deliver us from evil. Amen.

THE HAIL MARY

This prayer has three parts: 1) the greeting of the Angel Gabriel to Mary at the Annunciation (Luke 1:28), 2) the greeting of Elizabeth to Mary at the Visitation (Luke 1:42), and 3) a petition added by the Church.

Hail Mary, full of grace! the Lord is with Thee; blessed art Thou among women, and blessed is the fruit of Thy womb, Jesus. Holy Mary, Mother of God, pray for us sinners, now and at the hour of our death. Amen.

THE GLORY BE TO THE FATHER

The custom of adding a short formula of praise at the end of the other prayers was common in the synagogue, and has been adopted also by Christians. The Glory be to the Father is the customary form of praise with which Christian prayers are concluded.

Glory be to the Father, and to the Son, and to the Holy Ghost. As it was in the beginning, is now, and ever shall be, world without end. Amen.

HAIL, HOLY QUEEN

Hail, Holy Queen, Mother of Mercy, Hail, our life, our sweetness, and our hope! To Thee do we cry, poor banished children of Eve, to Thee do we send up our sighs, mourning and weeping in this valley of tears. Turn then, Most gracious Advocate, Thine eyes of mercy toward us; and after this our exile show unto us the blessed Fruit of Thy womb, Jesus. O clement, O loving, O sweet Virgin Mary!

P. Pray for us, O Holy Mother of God.

R. That we may be made worthy of the promises of Christ.

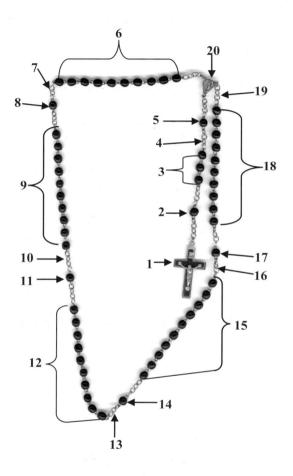

HOW TO RECITE THE ROSARY

1. Make the Sign of the Cross and say the Apostles' Creed.
2. Say the Our Father.
3. Say three Hail Marys.
4. Say the Glory be to the Father.
5. Announce the first mystery; then say the Our Father.
6. Say ten Hail Marys.
7. Say the Glory be to the Father & the Fatima Prayer.
8. Announce the second mystery; then say the Our Father.
9. Say ten Hail Marys.
10. Say the Glory be to the Father & the Fatima Prayer.
11. Announce the third mystery; then say the Our Father.
12. Say ten Hail Marys.
13. Say the Glory be to the Father & the Fatima Prayer.
14. Announce the fourth mystery; then say the Our Father.
15. Say ten Hail Marys.
16. Say the Glory be to the Father & the Fatima Prayer.
17. Announce the fifth mystery; then say the Our Father.
18. Say ten Hail Marys.
19. Say the Glory be to the Father & the Fatima Prayer.
20. Hail Holy Queen on the Medal.

ORIGIN AND METHOD
OF THE 54 DAY NOVENA

A NOVENA is nine days of public or private prayer to gain special graces. It originated in the nine days, after the Ascension of Christ, which Mary and the Disciples spent in prayer before the coming of the Holy Ghost.

A Rosary novena may be made at any time by simply saying the Rosary nine times, although gratitude demands that, if the favor asked for is granted, another novena should be made in thanksgiving.

Great impetus was given to the Rosary devotion in 1876, upon the erection of the sanctuary of Our Lady of the Rosary at Pompeii, Italy. The following is an illustration of one of the many graces granted.

Fortuna Agrelli, a Neapolitan girl, was hopelessly ill and suffering intense pain. Expert physicians declared her incurable. A novena of Rosaries was made by her and a few relatives beginning February 16, 1884. Fifteen days later she saw the Queen of the Rosary seated on a throne with the Infant Jesus in Her lap, a Rosary in Her hand, and accompanied by St. Dominic and St. Catherine of Siena.

"Child," said the Blessed Virgin, "you have invoked Me by many titles and have always obtained favors from Me. Now, since you have called Me by the title so pleasing to Me, 'Queen of the Holy Rosary,' I can no longer refuse the favor you ask, for this name is most precious and dear to Me. Make three novenas and you will obtain all." The girl obeyed and was perfectly cured.

Once more the Rosary Queen appeared to her and said: "Whoever desires to obtain favors from Me should make three novenas of the prayers of the Rosary in petition and three novenas in thanks.

This so-called IRRESISTIBLE NOVENA devotion which originated at the sanctuary of Our Lady of the Rosary of Pompeii is made by saying one Rosary of five decades every day for 54 consecutive days. In short, 54 Rosaries.

The Joyful Mysteries are recited on the first day, the Sorrowful Mysteries on the second day, and the Glorious Mysteries on the third day. This is repeated until 54 days have elapsed. The first three novenas, or 27 Rosaries, are recited in petition, and the last three novenas, or

27 Rosaries, are offered in thanksgiving. Eighteen complete Rosaries, or 270 decades, are recited in all.

It should be remembered, however, that the power of any novena lies in persevering prayer, and not in any magical combination of the number nine.

The prayers for the decades are composed mainly by St. Alphonsus de Liguori.

Behold the days come, saith the Lord, and I will raise up to David a just branch: and a King shall reign, and shall be wise: and shall execute judgement and justice in the earth.

Jeremias 23:5

THE JOYFUL MYSTERIES

Prayer before the recitation:
In the name of the Father,
and of the Son, and of the
Holy Ghost.
Amen.

Then say:
Hail Mary.

IN PETITION

Behold the end for which the Son of God will be born an Infant, to give Himself to us from His Childhood, and thus to draw to Himself our love. Why (writes St. Francis de Sales) does Jesus take the sweet and tender form of an Infant, if it be not to stimulate us to love Him and to confide in Him? St. Peter Chrysologus had said before, "Thus He willed to be born, because He wished to be loved."

Holy Mary, Mother of God! But if Thou art the Mother of God, Thou art also the Mother of our salvation, and of us poor sinners; since God became man to save sinners, and made Thee His Mother, that Thy prayers might have power to save any sinner. Hasten, then, O Mary, and pray for us, *now, and at the hour of our death.* Pray always.

O most beautiful Queen, we have no pretensions to see Thee on earth, but we do desire to go to see Thee in Paradise; and it is Thou who must obtain us this grace. For it we hope with confidence. Amen, amen. St. Alphonsus

*Creed, Our Father, 3 Hail Marys,
Glory be to the Father.*

I
THE ANNUNCIATION

O Immaculate and Holy Virgin! O Creature the most humble and the most exalted before God! Thou wast so lowly in Thine own eyes, but so great in the eyes of Thy Lord, that He exalted Thee to such a degree as to choose Thee for His Mother, and then made Thee Queen of Heaven and earth. I therefore thank God who so greatly has exalted Thee, and rejoice in seeing Thee so closely united with Him, that more cannot be granted to a pure creature.
I humbly pray: St. Alphonsus

Our Father

'I will put enmities between thee and the Woman
and thy seed and Her seed:
Genesis 3:15
Hail Mary

She shall crush thy head,
and thou shall lie in wait for Her heel.'
Genesis 3:15
Hail Mary

'Therefore the Lord Himself
shall give you a sign.
Isaias 7:14
Hail Mary

Behold a Virgin shall conceive, and bear a Son,
and His name shall be called Emanuel.'
Isaias 7:14
Hail Mary

The angel Gabriel was sent from God
to a Virgin espoused to a man whose name
was Joseph, and the Virgin's name was Mary.
Luke 1:26, 27
Hail Mary

'Hail, full of grace, the Lord is with Thee:
blessed art Thou among women.'
Luke 1:28
Hail Mary

'The Holy Ghost shall come upon Thee,
and the power of the most High shall overshadow Thee.'
Luke 1:35
Hail Mary

'And therefore also the Holy which shall be born
of Thee shall be called the Son of God.'
Luke 1:35
Hail Mary

'Thy cousin Elizabeth, she also hath conceived a son in
her old age. Because no word shall be impossible with God.'
Luke 1:36, 37
Hail Mary

And Mary said: 'Behold the Handmaid of the Lord;
be it done to Me according to Thy word.'
Luke 1:38
Hail Mary

Glory be to the Father

O my Jesus, forgive us, save us from the
fire of hell. Lead all souls to Heaven,
especially those who are most in need.

Queen of the Holy Rosary,
be gracious to me and grant me the grace of

HUMILITY

O great Mother of God; for I now understand that it is principally through the merits of Jesus Christ, and then through Thy intercession, that my soul must be saved. Ah! my Queen, Thou didst hasten so greatly to visit, and by that means didst sanctify the dwelling of St. Elizabeth: deign, then, to visit, and visit quickly, the poor house of my soul. I humbly pray: St. Alphonsus

Our Father

Mary rising up in those days, went into the hill country with haste. And She entered into the house of Zachary, and saluted Elizabeth.
Luke 1:39, 40
Hail Mary

When Elizabeth heard the salutation of Mary, the infant leaped in her womb. And Elizabeth was filled with the Holy Ghost.
Luke 1:41
Hail Mary

And Elizabeth cried out with a loud voice,
and said: 'Blessed art Thou among women,
and blessed is the Fruit of Thy womb.'
Luke 1:42
Hail Mary

'And whence is this to me, that the
Mother of my Lord should come to me?'
Luke 1:43
Hail Mary

'And blessed art Thou that hast believed,
because those things shall be accomplished
that were spoken to Thee by the Lord.'
Luke 1:45
Hail Mary

And Mary abode with her about three months;
and She returned to Her own house.
Luke 1:56
Hail Mary

Now Elizabeth's full time of being delivered
was come, and she brought forth a son.
Luke 1:57
Hail Mary

There was a man sent from God,
whose name was John.
John 1:6
Hail Mary

This man came for a witness, to give testimony
of the light, that all men might believe through him.
John 1:7
Hail Mary

He was not the light,
but was to give testimony of the light.
John 1:8
Hail Mary

Glory be to the Father

O my Jesus, forgive us, save us from the
fire of hell. Lead all souls to Heaven,
especially those who are most in need.

Queen of the Holy Rosary,
be gracious to me and grant me the grace of

CHARITY

Ⓞ my sweet, amiable, and Holy Child! Thou art at a loss what more to do to make Thyself beloved by men. It is enough to say that from being the Son of God Thou wert made the Son of Man, and that Thou chosest to be born among men like the rest of infants, only poorer and more meanly lodged than the rest, selecting a stable for Thy abode, a manger for Thy cradle, and a little straw for Thy couch. Thou didst desire thus to make Thy first appearance before us in the semblance of a poor child, that even from Thy very birth Thou mightest lose no time in attracting our hearts toward Thee. St. Alphonsus

I humbly pray:

Our Father

Mary was espoused to Joseph, before they came together, She was found with Child, of the Holy Ghost.
Matt. 1:18
Hail Mary

Joseph, being a just man, and not willing publicly to expose Her, was minded to put Her away privately.
Matt. 1:19
Hail Mary

Angel of the Lord appeared to him in his sleep,
'Joseph, son of David,
fear not to take unto thee Mary thy wife:'
Matt 1:20
Hail Mary

'For that which is conceived in Her,
is of the Holy Ghost. She shall bring forth a Son.'
Matt. 1:20, 21
Hail Mary

'And thou shalt call His name JESUS.
For He shall save His people from their sins.'
Matt. 1:21
Hail Mary

There went out a decree from Caesar Augustus,
that the whole world should be enrolled.
Luke 2:1
Hail Mary

Joseph went out of the city of Nazareth
to the city of David, which is called Bethlehem.
Luke 2:4
Hail Mary

It came to pass, that when they were in Bethlehem,
Her days were accomplished, that She should be delivered.
Luke 2:6
Hail Mary

And She brought forth Her firstborn Son,
and wrapped Him up in swaddling clothes.
Luke 2:7
Hail Mary

And laid Him in a manger;
because there was no room for them in the inn.
Luke 2:7
Hail Mary

Glory be to the Father

O my Jesus, forgive us, save us from the
fire of hell. Lead all souls to Heaven,
especially those who are most in need.

Queen of the Holy Rosary,
be gracious to me and grant me the grace of

DETACHMENT FROM THE WORLD

IV
THE PRESENTATION

Holy Mother of God, and my Mother Mary, Thou wast so deeply interested in my salvation as to offer to death the dearest object of Thy Heart, Thy beloved Jesus! Since, then Thou didst so much desire to see me saved, it is right that after God, I should place all my hopes in Thee. O yes, most Blessed Virgin, I do indeed entirely confide in Thee. I humbly pray: St. Alphonsus

Our Father

For a CHILD IS BORN to us, and a Son is given to us,
and His name shall be called the Prince of Peace.
Isaias 9:6
Hail Mary

According to the law of Moses, they carried
Him to Jerusalem, to present Him to the Lord.
Luke 2:22
Hail Mary

Behold there was a man in Jerusalem named Simeon,
and this man was just and devout,
waiting for the consolation of Israel.
Luke 2:25
Hail Mary

And he received an answer from the Holy Ghost, that he
should not see death, before he had seen the Christ of the Lord.
Luke 2:26
Hail Mary

And when His parents brought in the Child Jesus, Simeon
also took Him into his arms, and blessed God and said:
Luke 2:27, 28
Hail Mary

'Now Thou dost dismiss Thy servant, O Lord,
according to Thy word, in peace.'
Luke 2:29
Hail Mary

'Because my eyes have seen Thy salvation,
which Thou hast prepared before the face of all peoples:'
Luke 2:30, 31
Hail Mary

'A Light to the revelation of the Gentiles,
and the Glory of Thy people Israel.'
Luke 2:32
Hail Mary

And said to Mary His Mother: 'Behold this Child is set for
the fall, and for the resurrection of many in Israel,
and for a sign which shall be contradicted.'
Luke 2:34
Hail Mary

'And Thy own soul a sword shall pierce,
that, out of many hearts, thoughts may be revealed.'
Luke 2:35
Hail Mary

Glory be to the Father

O my Jesus, forgive us, save us from the
fire of hell. Lead all souls to Heaven,
especially those who are most in need.

Queen of the Holy Rosary,
be gracious to me and grant me the grace of

OBEDIENCE

V
THE FINDING OF THE CHILD JESUS IN THE TEMPLE

Mary, Thou weepest because Thou hast lost Thy Son for a few days; He has withdrawn Himself from Thy eyes, but not from Thy Heart. O my Jesus, I desire not to lose Thee anymore; but I cannot trust to myself, I trust in Thee. I beseech Thee, do Thou bind me to Thee, and permit me not to be again separated from Thee. O Mary! through Thee have I found my God, whom I had once lost; do Thou obtain for me also holy perseverance; wherefore I will also say to Thee with St. Bonaventure, *In Thee, O Lady, have I hoped; let me not be confounded forever.*   St. Alphonsus
I humbly pray:

Our Father

When Jesus was twelve years old, they going up into Jerusalem according to the custom of the feast.
Luke 2:42
Hail Mary

When they returned, the Child Jesus remained in Jerusalem; and His parents knew it not.
Luke 2:43
Hail Mary

They returned into Jerusalem, seeking Him.
After three days, they found Him in the temple,
Luke 2:45, 46
Hail Mary

sitting in the midst of the doctors,
hearing them, and asking them questions.
Luke 2:46
Hail Mary

And all that heard Him were astonished
at His wisdom and His answers.
Luke 2:47
Hail Mary

'Son, why hast Thou done so to us?
Behold Thy father and I have sought Thee sorrowing.'
Luke 2:48
Hail Mary

'How is it that You sought Me? Did You not
know, that I must be about My Father's business?'
Luke 2:49
Hail Mary

And they understood not
the word that He spoke unto them.
Luke 2:50
Hail Mary

And He went down with them, and came to Nazareth,
and was subject to them.
Luke 2:51
Hail Mary

And Jesus advanced in wisdom, and age,
and grace with God and men.
Luke 2:52
Hail Mary

Glory be to the Father

O my Jesus, forgive us, save us from the
fire of hell. Lead all souls to Heaven,
especially those who are most in need.

Queen of the Holy Rosary,
be gracious to me and grant me the grace of

PIETY

Closing Prayers, page 84

If the world hate you, know ye, that it hath hated Me before you. The servant is not greater than his master. If they have persecuted Me, they will also persecute you.

John 15:18, 20

THE SORROWFUL MYSTERIES

Prayer before the recitation:
In the name of the Father,
and of the Son, and of the
Holy Ghost.
Amen.

Then say:
Hail Mary.

IN PETITION

O my Jesus! I pray Thee make me always remember Thy Passion; and grant that I also, a miserable sinner, overcome at last by so many loving devices, may return to love Thee, and to show Thee, by my poor love, some mark of gratitude for the excessive love which Thou, my God and my Saviour, hast borne to me.

And Thou, O most holy Virgin Mary, who didst take so great a part in the Passion of Thy Son, obtain for me, I beseech Thee, through the merits of Thy sorrows, the grace to experience a taste of that compassion which Thou didst so sensibly feel at the death of Jesus, and obtain for me also a spark of that love which wrought all the martyrdom of Thy afflicted heart.

O most beautiful Queen, we have no pretensions to see Thee on earth, but we do desire to go to see Thee in Paradise; and it is Thou who must obtain us this grace. For it we hope with confidence. Amen, amen. St. Alphonsus

Creed, Our Father, 3 Hail Marys,
Glory be to the Father.

I
THE AGONY

O my Jesus, it is not the executioners, the scourges, the thorns, or the cross that have been so cruel: the cruelty lies in my sins, which afflicted Thee so much in the garden. Do Thou give me, then, a share of that sorrow and abhorrence which Thou didst experience in the garden, that so, even to my death, I may bitterly weep for the offences that I have given Thee. I love Thee, O my Jesus: do Thou receive with kindness a sinner who wishes to love Thee. Recommend me, O Mary, to this thy Son, who is in affliction and sadness for love of me. St. Alphonsus

I humbly pray:

Our Father

Jesus came with them into Gethsemani,
and He began to grow sorrowful and to be sad.
Matt. 26:36, 37
Hail Mary

Then He saith to them, 'My soul is sorrowful even unto death.
Pray lest ye enter into temptation.'
Matt. 26:38 / *Luke* 22:40
Hail Mary

And He was withdrawn away from them a stone's cast;
and kneeling down He prayed.
Luke 22:41
Hail Mary

'Abba, Father, all things are possible to Thee: remove this chalice
from Me; but not what I will, but what Thou wilt.'
Mark 14:36
Hail Mary

And there appeared to Him an angel
from Heaven, strengthening Him.
Luke 22:43
Hail Mary

And being in an agony He prayed the longer.
Luke 22:43
Hail Mary

And His sweat became as drops of blood
trickling down upon the ground.
Luke 22:44
Hail Mary

And He cometh to His disciples, and findeth them asleep,
and He said, 'What? Could you not watch one hour with Me?'
Matt. 26:40
Hail Mary

'Watch ye, and pray, that ye enter not into temptation.
The spirit indeed is willing, but the flesh weak.'
Matt. 26:41
Hail Mary

And going away again, He prayed,
saying the same words.
Mark 14:39
Hail Mary
Glory be to the Father.

O my Jesus, forgive us, save us from the
fire of hell. Lead all souls to Heaven,
especially those who are most in need.

Queen of the Holy Rosary,
be gracious to me and grant me the grace of

RESIGNATION TO THE WILL OF GOD

II
THE SCOURGING

My beloved Saviour, I behold Thee all torn in pieces for me; no longer, therefore, can I doubt that Thou dost love me, and love me greatly, too. Every wound of Thine is a sure token on Thy part of Thy love, which with too much reason demands my love. Thou, O my Jesus, dost, without reserve, give me Thy blood; it is but just that I, without reserve, should give Thee all my heart. Do Thou, then, accept of it, and make it to be ever faithful.

St. Alphonsus

I humbly pray:

Our Father

The high priest said to Him: 'I adjure Thee by the living God, that Thou tell us if Thou be the Christ the Son of God.'
Matt. 26:63
Hail Mary

'I am. And you shall see the Son of Man
sitting on the right hand of the power of God,
and coming with the clouds of Heaven.'
Mark 14:62
Hail Mary

Binding Jesus, led Him away, and delivered Him to Pilate.
And Pilate asked Him, 'Art thou the king of the Jews?'
Mark 15:1, 2
Hail Mary

Jesus answered, 'My kingdom is not of this world.
Thou sayest that I am a king.'
John 18:36, 37
Hail Mary

'For this was I born, and for this came I into the world;
That I should give testimony to the truth.'
John 18:37
Hail Mary

'Every one that is of the truth, heareth My voice.'
Pilate saith to Him: 'What is truth?'
John 18:37, 38
Hail Mary

Then Pilate said, 'I find no cause in this Man.
I will chastise Him therefore, and release Him.'
Luke 23:4, 16
Hail Mary

Then therefore Pilate took Jesus
and scourged Him.
John 19:1
Hail Mary

He was wounded for our iniquities,
He was bruised for our sins.
Isaias 53:5
Hail Mary

The chastisement of our peace was upon Him,
and by His bruises we are healed.
Isaias 53:5
Hail Mary

Glory be to the Father.

O my Jesus, forgive us, save us from the
fire of hell. Lead all souls to Heaven,
especially those who are most in need.

Queen of the Holy Rosary,
be gracious to me and grant me the grace of

PURITY

THE CROWNING WITH THORNS

*T*his vile crowd, not content with having so barbarously crowned Jesus Christ, wished to mock Him, and to multiply fresh insults and torments; and so they bent the knee before Him, and deridingly saluted Him, "Hail, King of the Jews;" they spat in His face, they struck Him with the palms of their hands; with cries and ridicule and contempt they vilely insult Him. *St. Alphonsus*

I humbly pray:

Our Father

And the soldiers led Him away into the court of the palace, and they called together the whole band.
Mark 15:16
Hail Mary

And stripping Him,
they put a scarlet cloak about Him.
Matt. 27:28
Hail Mary

And platting a crown of thorns, they put it upon
His head, and a reed in His right hand.
Matt. 27:29
Hail Mary

And bowing the knee before Him, they mocked Him,
saying: 'Hail, King of the Jews!'
Matt. 27:29
Hail Mary

And spitting upon Him,
they took the reed, and struck His head.
Matt. 27:30
Hail Mary

All they that saw Me have laughed Me to scorn;
they have spoken with the lips, and wagged the head.
Psalm 21:8
Hail Mary

Pilate therefore went forth again, and saith to them:
'Behold, I bring Him forth unto you,
that you may know that I find no cause in Him.'
John 19:4
Hail Mary

Jesus therefore came forth, bearing
the crown of thorns and the purple garment.
John 19:5
Hail Mary

And Pilate said to them, 'Behold the Man.'
But they cried out, 'Away with Him;
away with Him; Crucify Him.'
John 19:5, 15
Hail Mary

They have opened their mouths against Me,
as a lion ravening and roaring.
Psalm 21:14
Hail Mary

Glory be to the Father.

O my Jesus, forgive us, save us from the
fire of hell. Lead all souls to Heaven,
especially those who are most in need.

Queen of the Holy Rosary,
be gracious to me and grant me the grace of

HUMILITY

IV
THE CARRYING OF THE CROSS

O my Redeemer! by the merits of this sorrowful journey of Thine, give me strength to bear my cross with patience. I accept of all the sufferings and contempts which Thou dost destine for me to undergo. Thou hast rendered them lovely and sweet by embracing them for love of us: give me strength to endure them with calmness.   St. Alphonsus

I humbly pray:

Our Father

And he took the wood for the holocaust,
and laid it upon Isaac his son.
Gen. 22:6
Hail Mary

He humbled Himself, becoming obedient unto death,
even to the death of the cross.
Phil. 2:8
Hail Mary

And bearing His own cross,
He went forth to that place which is called Calvary.
John 19:17
Hail Mary

Surely He hath borne our infirmities
and carried our sorrows:
Isaias 53:4
Hail Mary

'If any man will come after Me, let him deny himself.'
Luke 9:23
Hail Mary

'And take up his cross daily, and follow Me.'
Luke 9:23
Hail Mary

And thou hast brought Me down into the dust of death.
Psalm 21:16
Hail Mary

And they laid hold of one Simon of Cyrene,
and they laid the cross on him to carry after Jesus.
Luke 23:26
Hail Mary

'Take up My yoke upon you, and learn of Me,
because I am meek, and humble of heart:'
Matt. 11:29
Hail Mary

'And you shall find rest to your souls.
For My yoke is sweet and My burden light.'
Matt. 11:29, 30
Hail Mary

Glory be to the Father.

O my Jesus, forgive us, save us from the
fire of hell. Lead all souls to Heaven,
especially those who are most in need.

Queen of the Holy Rosary,
be gracious to me and grant me the grace of

PATIENCE IN ADVERSITY

O God! who shall not compassionate the Son of God, who for love of men is dying of grief on a cross? He is tormented externally in His body by the innumerable wounds, and internally He is so afflicted and sad that He seeks solace for His great sorrow from the Eternal Father; but His Father, in order to satisfy His divine justice, abandons Him, and leaves Him to die desolate and deprived of every consolation.
I humbly pray: St. Alphonsus

Our Father

And when they were come to the
place which is called Calvary,
they crucified Him there.
Luke 23:33
Hail Mary

They parted My garments amongst them;
and upon My vesture they cast lots.
Psalm 21:19
Hail Mary

The chief priests mocking said:
'He saved others; Himself He cannot save.
Matt. 27:41, 42
Hail Mary

He trusted in God; let Him now deliver Him if He will
have Him; for He said: I am the Son of God.'
Matt. 27:43
Hail Mary

And Jesus said, 'Father, forgive them,
for they know not what they do.'
Luke 23:34
Hail Mary

And one of the robbers hanged with Him said, 'Lord,
remember Me when thou shalt come into Thy kingdom.'
Luke 23:39, 42
Hail Mary

And Jesus said to him, 'Amen I say to thee,
this day thou shalt be with Me in Paradise.'
Luke 23:43
Hail Mary

When Jesus therefore had seen His Mother
and the disciple standing whom He loved,
John 19:26
Hail Mary

He saith to His Mother, 'Woman, behold, Thy son.'
After that, He saith to the disciple, 'Behold, thy Mother.'
John 19:26, 27
Hail Mary

And from that hour,
the disciple took Her to his own.
John 19:27
Hail Mary

Glory be to the Father.

O my Jesus, forgive us, save us from the
fire of hell. Lead all souls to Heaven,
especially those who are most in need.

Queen of the Holy Rosary,
be gracious to me and grant me the grace of

LOVE OF OUR ENEMIES

Closing Prayers, page 84

*L*et God arise, and let His enemies be scattered: and let them that hate Him flee from before His face.

Psalm 67:2

THE GLORIOUS MYSTERIES

Prayer before the recitation:
In the name of the Father, and
of the Son, and of the
Holy Ghost.
Amen.

Then say:
Hail Mary.

IN PETITION

Your sorrow (says the Saviour, to encourage us) shall be turned into joy. Ah, my God, I deserve not paradise, but hell; yet Thy death gives me a hope of obtaining it. I desire and ask Paradise of Thee, not so much in order to enjoy, as in order to love Thee everlastingly, secure that it will never more be possible for me to lose Thee.

Lady, do Thou pray for me, for Thou wilt ask for the graces I require with greater devotion than I can dare to ask for them; and Thou wilt obtain far greater graces from God for me than I can presume to seek.

most beautiful Queen, we have no pretensions to see Thee on earth, but we do desire to go to see Thee in Paradise; and it is Thou who must obtain us this grace. For it we hope with confidence. Amen, amen. St. Alphonsus

Creed, Our Father, 3 Hail Marys,
Glory be to the Father.

I
THE RESURRECTION

J esus, Thou didst rise again the third day. I beseech
Thee by Thy resurrection, make me rise glorious
with Thee at the last day, to be always united with Thee
in Heaven, to praise Thee and love Thee forever.
I humbly pray: St. Alphonsus

Our Father

Mary Magdalen, and Mary the mother of James, and
Salome bought sweet spices, they might anoint Jesus.
Mark 16:1
Hail Mary

And looking, they saw the stone rolled back.
For it was very great.
Mark 16:4
Hail Mary

Mary Magdalen ran to Simon Peter
and to the other disciple whom Jesus loved.
John 20:2
Hail Mary

'They have taken away the Lord out of the sepulchre,
and we know not where they have laid Him.'
John 20:2
Hail Mary

But Mary Magdalen stood
at the sepulchre without, weeping.
Angels said to her: 'Woman, why weepest thou?'
John 20:11, 13
Hail Mary

She saith to them: 'Because they have taken away
my Lord; and I know not where they have laid Him.'
John 20:13
Hail Mary

Jesus saith to her: 'Woman, why weepest thou?
Whom seekest thou?'
John 20:15
Hail Mary

'Sir, if thou hast taken Him hence, tell me where
thou hast laid Him, and I will take Him away.'
John 20:15
Hail Mary

Jesus saith to her: 'Mary.' She turning
saith to Him: 'Rabboni' (which is to say, Master).
John 20:16
Hail Mary

Jesus saith to her: 'Do not touch Me,
for I am not yet ascended to My Father.'
John 20:17
Hail Mary

Glory be to the Father.

O my Jesus, forgive us, save us from the
fire of hell. Lead all souls to Heaven,
especially those who are most in need.

Queen of the Holy Rosary,
be gracious to me and grant me the grace of

FAITH

II
THE ASCENSION

Ah, my God, make me love Thee exceedingly in this life, that I may love Thee exceedingly in eternity. Thou art the object most worthy of being loved; Thou dost deserve all my love: I will love none but Thee. Do Thou help me by Thy grace. I humbly pray:
                                                              St. Alphonsus

Our Father

The eleven disciples went into Galilee,
unto the mountain where Jesus had appointed them.
Matt. 28:16
Hail Mary

And seeing Him they adored:
but some doubted.
Matt. 28:17
Hail Mary

And Jesus coming, spoke to them, saying:
'All power is given to Me in Heaven and in earth.'
Matt. 28:18
Hail Mary

'Going therefore, teach ye all nations; Baptizing them in the
name of the Father, and of the Son, and of the Holy Ghost.'
Matt. 28:19
Hail Mary

'Go ye into the whole world,
and preach the gospel to every creature.'
Mark 16:15
Hail Mary

'Teaching them to observe
all things whatsoever I have commanded you.'
Matt. 28:20
Hail Mary

'And behold, I am with you all days,
even unto the consummation of the world.'
Matt. 28:20
Hail Mary

And the Lord Jesus was taken up into Heaven,
and sitteth on the right hand of God.
Mark 16:19
Hail Mary

But there are also many other things which Jesus did;
which, if they were written every one,
John 21:25
Hail Mary

the world itself, I think, would not be able to contain
the books that should be written.
John 21:25
Hail Mary

Glory be to the Father.

O my Jesus, forgive us, save us from the
fire of hell. Lead all souls to Heaven,
especially those who are most in need.

Queen of the Holy Rosary,
be gracious to me and grant me the grace of

HOPE

III
THE DESCENT OF THE HOLY GHOST

C ome, Holy Ghost, Sanctifier all powerful, God of love, Thou who didst fill the Virgin Mary with grace, Thou who didst wonderfully transform the hearts of the Apostles, Thou who didst endow all Thy martyrs with a miraculous heroism, come and sanctify us. Illumine our minds, strengthen our will, purify our consciences, rectify our judgments, set our hearts on fire, and preserve us from the misfortune of resisting Thine inspirations. I humbly pray:

Unknown

Our Father

'I will ask the Father, and He shall give you another Paraclete, that He may abide with you forever.'
John 14:16
Hail Mary

'The Spirit of truth, you shall know Him;
because He shall abide with you, and shall be in you.'
John 14:17
Hail Mary

'But the Paraclete, the Holy Ghost, whom the Father
will send in My name, He will teach you all things,
John 14:26
Hail Mary

and bring all things to your mind,
whatsoever I shall have said to you.'
John 14:26
Hail Mary

'It is expedient to you that I go:
for if I go not, the Paraclete will not come to you;
John 16:7
Hail Mary

But if I go, I will send Him to you.'
John 16:7
Hail Mary

They went up into an upper room, now the number of
persons together was about a hundred and twenty.
Acts 1:13, 15
Hail Mary

And when the days of the Pentecost
were accomplished, suddenly there came a sound
from Heaven, as of a mighty wind coming.
Acts 2:1, 2
Hail Mary

And there appeared to them parted tongues as it
were of fire, and it sat upon every one of them.
Acts 2:3
Hail Mary

And they were all filled with the Holy Ghost.
Acts 2:4
Hail Mary

Glory be to the Father.

O my Jesus, forgive us, save us from the
fire of hell. Lead all souls to Heaven,
especially those who are most in need.

Queen of the Holy Rosary,
be gracious to me and grant me the grace of

CHARITY

IV
THE ASSUMPTION OF OUR BLESSED MOTHER INTO HEAVEN

O Immaculate Virgin, Mother of God and Mother of men. We believe with all the fervor of our faith in Thy triumphal Assumption, both in body and soul, into Heaven, where Thou are acclaimed as Queen by all the choirs of angels and all the legions of saints; and we unite with them to praise and bless the Lord who has exalted Thee above all other pure creatures, and to offer Thee the tribute of our devotion and our love.

Pius XII

I humbly pray:

Our Father

Arise, My love, My beautiful one, and come:
for Thy voice is sweet, and Thy face comely.
Cant. 2:13, 14
Hail Mary

Blessed art Thou, O Daughter, by the Lord the
most high God, above all women upon earth.
Judith 13:23
Hail Mary

Because He hath so magnified Thy name this day,
that Thy praise shall not depart out of the mouth of men.
Judith 13:25
Hail Mary

In every nation which shall hear Thy name, the God
of Israel shall be magnified on occasion of Thee.
Judith 13:31
Hail Mary

Thou art the Glory of Jerusalem, Thou art the
Joy of Israel, Thou art the Honor of our people.
Judith 15:10
Hail Mary

They shall remember Thy name throughout all generations.
Psalm 44:18
Hail Mary

Therefore shall people praise Thee for ever;
yea, for ever and ever.
Psalm 44:18
Hail Mary

I will greatly rejoice in the Lord,
and My soul shall be joyful in My God:
Isaias 61:10
Hail Mary

for He hath clothed Me with the garments of salvation:
Isaias 61:10
Hail Mary

and with the robe of justice He hath covered Me,
as a bride adorned with her jewels.
Isaias 61:10
Hail Mary

Glory be to the Father.

O my Jesus, forgive us, save us from the
fire of hell. Lead all souls to Heaven,
especially those who are most in need.

Queen of the Holy Rosary,
be gracious to me and grant me the grace of

UNION WITH CHRIST

V
THE CORONATION OF OUR BLESSED
MOTHER IN HEAVEN AS ITS QUEEN

O great, exalted, and most glorious Lady, prostrate at the foot of Thy throne we adore Thee from this valley of tears. We rejoice at Thy immense glory, with which our Lord has enriched Thee; and now that Thou art enthroned as Queen of Heaven and earth, ah forget us not, Thy poor servants. Disdain not, from the high throne on which Thou reignest, to cast Thine eyes of mercy on us miserable creatures. The nearer Thou art to the source of graces, in the greater abundance canst Thou procure those graces for us.   St. Alphonsus

I humbly pray:

Our Father

And the temple of God was opened in Heaven:
and there were of lightnings, and voices...
Apoc. 11:19
Hail Mary

And a great sign appeared in Heaven:
a Woman clothed with the sun.
Apoc. 12:1
Hail Mary

And the moon under Her feet,
and on Her head a crown of twelve stars.
Apoc. 12:1
Hail Mary

And the King loved Her more than all the women,
and She had favour and kindness before Him
above all the women,
Esther 2:17
Hail Mary

and He set the royal crown on Her head,
and made Her Queen.
Esther 2:17
Hail Mary

The Queen stood on Thy right hand, in gilded clothing;
surrounded with variety,
Psalm 44:10
Hail Mary

I am the Mother of fair love, and of fear,
and of knowledge, and of holy hope.
Ecclus. 24:24
Hail Mary

Now therefore, ye children, hear Me:
Blessed are they that keep My ways.
Prov. 8:32
Hail Mary

Hear instruction and be wise, and refuse it not.
Blessed is the man that heareth Me.
Prov. 8:33, 34
Hail Mary

He that shall find Me, shall find life,
and shall have salvation from the Lord.
Prov. 8:35
Hail Mary

Glory be to the Father.

O my Jesus, forgive us, save us from the
fire of hell. Lead all souls to Heaven,
especially those who are most in need.

Queen of the Holy Rosary,
be gracious to me and grant me the grace of
UNION WITH THEE

Closing Prayers, page 84

Behold the Lamb of God, behold Him who taketh away the sin of the world.

John 1:29

THE JOYFUL MYSTERIES

Prayer before the recitation:
In the name of the Father,
and of the Son, and of the
Holy Ghost.
Amen.

Then say:
Hail Mary.

IN THANKSGIVING

Behold the end for which the Son of God will be born an Infant, to give Himself to us from His Childhood, and thus to draw to Himself our love. Why (writes St. Francis de Sales) does Jesus take the sweet and tender form of an Infant, if it be not to stimulate us to love Him and to confide in Him? St. Peter Chrysologus had said before, "Thus He willed to be born, because He wished to be loved."

Holy Mary, Mother of God! But if Thou art the Mother of God, Thou art also the Mother of our salvation, and of us poor sinners; since God became man to save sinners, and made Thee His Mother, that Thy prayers might have power to save any sinner. Hasten, then, O Mary, and pray for us, *now, and at the hour of our death.* Pray always.   St. Alphonsus

Queen of the Holy Rosary, I give Thee my heart in thanksgiving for this favor.

Creed, Our Father, 3 Hail Marys,
Glory be to the Father.

I
THE ANNUNCIATION

Immaculate and Holy Virgin! O Creature the most humble and the most exalted before God! Thou wast so lowly in Thine own eyes, but so great in the eyes of Thy Lord, that He exalted Thee to such a degree as to choose Thee for His Mother, and then made Thee Queen of Heaven and earth. I therefore thank God who so greatly has exalted Thee, and rejoice in seeing Thee so closely united with Him, that more cannot be granted to a pure creature.

I humbly pray:

St. Alphonsus

Our Father

The angel Gabriel was sent from God to a Virgin
espoused to a man whose name was Joseph,
and the Virgin's name was Mary.
Luke 1:26, 27
Hail Mary

'Hail, full of grace, the Lord is with Thee:
blessed art Thou among women.'
Luke 1:28
Hail Mary

Who having heard, was troubled at his saying, and
thought with Herself what manner of salutation this should be.
Luke 1:29
Hail Mary

And the angel said to Her, 'Fear not, Mary,
for Thou hast found grace with God.'
Luke 1:30
Hail Mary

'Behold, Thou shalt conceive in Thy womb, and shalt
bring forth a Son; and Thou shalt call His name Jesus.'
Luke 1:31
Hail Mary

'He shall be great,
and shall be called the Son of the most High;
And of His Kingdom there shall be no end.'
Luke 1:32, 33
Hail Mary

Mary said to the angel, 'How shall this be done,
because I know not man?'
Luke 1:34
Hail Mary

'The Holy Ghost shall come upon Thee
and the power of the most High shall overshadow Thee.'
Luke 1:35
Hail Mary

'And therefore also the Holy which shall be born of Thee
shall be called the Son of God.'
Luke 1:35
Hail Mary

And Mary said: 'Behold the Handmaid of the Lord;
be it done to Me according to thy word.'
Luke 1:38
Hail Mary

Glory be to the Father

O my Jesus, forgive us, save us from the
fire of hell. Lead all souls to Heaven,
especially those who are most in need.

Queen of the Holy Rosary,
be gracious to me and grant me the grace of

HUMILITY

II
THE VISITATION

O great Mother of God; for I now understand that it is principally through the merits of Jesus Christ, and then through Thy intercession, that my soul must be saved. Ah! my Queen, Thou didst hasten so greatly to visit, and by that means didst sanctify the dwelling of St. Elizabeth: deign, then, to visit, and visit quickly, the poor house of my soul.
I humbly pray:

St. Alphonsus

Our Father

Mary rising up in those days, went into the hill country with haste. And She entered into the house of Zachary, and saluted Elizabeth.
Luke 1:39, 40
Hail Mary

And Elizabeth cried out with a loud voice, and said:
'Blessed art Thou among women,
and blessed is the Fruit of Thy womb.'
Luke 1:42
Hail Mary

Mary said, 'My soul doth magnify the Lord.
And My spirit hath rejoiced in God My Savior.
Because He hath regarded the humility of His handmaid.'
Luke 1:46-48
Hail Mary

'For, behold from henceforth all generations shall call Me
blessed. Because He that is mighty,
hath done great things to Me.'
Luke 1:48, 49
Hail Mary

'And holy is His name; and His mercy is from
generation unto generations, to them that fear Him.'
Luke 1:49, 50
Hail Mary

'He hath shewed might in His arm, He
hath scattered the proud in the conceit of their heart.'
Luke 1:51
Hail Mary

'He hath put down the mighty from
their seat, and hath exalted the humble.'
Luke 1:52
Hail Mary

'He hath filled the hungry with good things;
and the rich He hath sent empty away.'
Luke 1:53
Hail Mary

'He hath received Israel His servant,
being mindful of His mercy.'
Luke 1:54
Hail Mary

'As He spoke to our fathers,
to Abraham and to his seed for ever.'
Luke 1:55
Hail Mary

Glory be to the Father

O my Jesus, forgive us, save us from the
fire of hell. Lead all souls to Heaven,
especially those who are most in need.

Queen of the Holy Rosary,
be gracious to me and grant me the grace of

CHARITY

III
THE NATIVITY

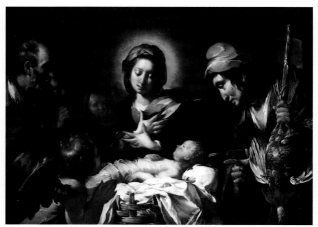

O my sweet, amiable, and Holy Child! Thou art at a loss what more to do to make Thyself beloved by men. It is enough to say that from being the Son of God Thou wert made the Son of Man, and that Thou chosest to be born among men like the rest of infants, only poorer and more meanly lodged than the rest, selecting a stable for Thy abode, a manger for Thy cradle, and a little straw for Thy couch. Thou didst desire thus to make Thy first appearance before us in the semblance of a poor child, that even from Thy very birth Thou mightest lose no time in attracting our hearts toward Thee.   St. Alphonsus
I humbly pray:

Our Father

And there were in the same country shepherds watching.
And behold an angel of the Lord stood by them.
Luke 2:8, 9
Hail Mary

'Fear not; for, behold,
I bring you good tidings of great joy,
that shall be to all the people:'
Luke 2:10
Hail Mary

'For this day, is born to you a Savior,
who is Christ the Lord, in the city of David.'
Luke 2:11
Hail Mary

'You shall find the Infant wrapped in swaddling clothes,
and laid in a manger.'
Luke 2:12
Hail Mary

And suddenly there was with the angel a multitude
of the Heavenly army, praising God, and saying:
Luke 2:13
Hail Mary

'Glory to God in the highest;
and on earth peace to men of good will.'
Luke 2:14
Hail Mary

The shepherds said, 'Let us go over to Bethlehem,
and let us see this word that is come to pass,
which the Lord hath shewed to us.'
Luke 2:15
Hail Mary

They came with haste; and they found Mary and Joseph,
and the Infant lying in the manger.
Luke 2:16
Hail Mary

And seeing, they understood of the word
that had been spoken to them concerning this Child.
Luke 2:17
Hail Mary

But Mary kept all these words,
pondering them in Her heart.
Luke 2:19
Hail Mary

Glory be to the Father

O my Jesus, forgive us, save us from the
fire of hell. Lead all souls to Heaven,
especially those who are most in need.

Queen of the Holy Rosary,
be gracious to me and grant me the grace of

DETACHMENT FROM THE WORLD

IV
THE PRESENTATION

O holy Mother of God, and my Mother Mary,
Thou wast so deeply interested in my salvation
as to offer to death the dearest object of Thy Heart,
Thy beloved Jesus! Since, then Thou didst so much
desire to see me saved, it is right that after God, I
should place all my hopes in Thee. O yes, most
Blessed Virgin, I do indeed entirely confide in Thee.
I humbly pray: St. Alphonsus

Our Father

The prophet Simeon said 'Now thou dost dismiss
Thy servant, O Lord, according to Thy word, in peace.'
Luke 2:29
Hail Mary

'Because my eyes have seen Thy salvation,
which Thou hast prepared before the face of all peoples.'
Luke 2:30, 31
Hail Mary

And there was one Anna, a prophetess,
she was far advanced in years.
Luke 2:36
Hail Mary

She was a widow
until fourscore and four years.
Luke 2:37
Hail Mary

Anna departed not from the temple,
by fastings and prayers serving night and day.
Luke 2:37
Hail Mary

Now she, coming in, confessed to the Lord; and spoke
of Him to all that looked for the redemption of Israel.
Luke 2:38
Hail Mary

That every tongue should confess that the
Lord Jesus Christ is in the glory of God the Father.
Phil 2:11
Hail Mary

Behold an angel of the Lord appeared in sleep to
Joseph, saying: 'Arise, and take the Child and His Mother,'
Matt 2:13
Hail Mary

'And fly into Egypt: and be there until I shall tell thee.
For it will come to pass that Herod will seek
the Child to destroy Him.'
Matt 2:13
Hail Mary

Joseph arose, and took the Child and His Mother
by night, and retired into Egypt:
and He was there until the death of Herod.
Matt 2:14
Hail Mary

Glory be to the Father

O my Jesus, forgive us, save us from the
fire of hell. Lead all souls to Heaven,
especially those who are most in need.

Queen of the Holy Rosary,
be gracious to me and grant me the grace of

OBEDIENCE

V
THE FINDING OF THE CHILD
JESUS IN THE TEMPLE

O Mary, Thou weepest because Thou hast lost Thy Son for a few days; He has withdrawn Himself from Thy eyes, but not from Thy Heart. O my Jesus, I desire not to lose Thee anymore; but I cannot trust to myself, I trust in Thee. I beseech Thee, do Thou bind me to Thee, and permit me not to be again separated from Thee. O Mary! through Thee have I found my God, whom I had once lost; do Thou obtain for me also holy perseverance; wherefore I will also say to Thee with St. Bonaventure, *In Thee, O Lady, have I hoped; let me not be confounded forever.*   St. Alphonsus
I humbly pray:

Our Father

When Jesus was twelve years old, they going up into
Jerusalem according to the custom of the feast.
Luke 2:42
Hail Mary

When they returned, the Child Jesus remained in
Jerusalem; and His parents knew it not.
Luke 2:43
Hail Mary

They returned into Jerusalem, seeking Him.
Have you seen Him, whom My soul loveth?
Luke 2:45 / *Cant.* 3:3
Hail Mary

And after three days, they found Him in the temple.
Luke 2:46
Hail Mary

The wisdom of the humble shall exalt His head,
and shall make Him sit in the midst of great men.
Ecclus. 11:1
Hail Mary

I have loved, O Lord, the beauty of Thy house:
and the place where Thy glory dwelleth.
Psalm 25:8
Hail Mary

'Son, why hast Thou done so to us? Behold,
Thy father and I have sought Thee sorrowing.'
Luke 2:48
Hail Mary

'How is it that You sought Me?
Did You not know,
that I must be about My Father's business?'
Luke 2:49
Hail Mary

And they understood not
the word that He spoke unto them.
Luke 2:50
Hail Mary

And He went down with them, and was subject to them.
And His Mother kept all these words in Her heart.
Luke 2:51
Hail Mary

Glory be to the Father

O my Jesus, forgive us, save us from the
fire of hell. Lead all souls to Heaven,
especially those who are most in need.

Queen of the Holy Rosary,
be gracious to me and grant me the grace of

PIETY

Closing Prayers, page 84

I lay down My life, that I may take it again. No man taketh it away from Me: but I lay it down of Myself, and I have power to lay it down: and I have power to take it up again. This commandment have I received of My Father.

John 10:17, 18

THE SORROWFUL MYSTERIES

Prayer before the recitation:
In the name of the Father, and
of the Son, and of the
Holy Ghost.
Amen.

Then say:
Hail Mary.

IN THANKSGIVING

O my Jesus! I pray Thee make me always remember Thy Passion; and grant that I also, a miserable sinner, overcome at last by so many loving devices, may return to love Thee, and to show Thee, by my poor love, some mark of gratitude for the excessive love which Thou, my God and my Saviour, hast borne to me.

And Thou, O most holy Virgin Mary, who didst take so great a part in the Passion of Thy Son, obtain for me, I beseech Thee, through the merits of Thy sorrows, the grace to experience a taste of that compassion which Thou didst so sensibly feel at the death of Jesus, and obtain for me also a spark of that love which wrought all the martyrdom of Thy afflicted heart. St. Alphonsus

Queen of the Holy Rosary, I give Thee my heart in thanksgiving for this favor.

Creed, Our Father, 3 Hail Marys,
Glory be to the Father.

I
THE AGONY

O my Jesus, it is not the executioners, the scourges, the thorns, or the cross that have been so cruel: the cruelty lies in my sins, which afflicted Thee so much in the garden. Do Thou give me, then, a share of that sorrow and abhorrence which Thou didst experience in the garden, that so, even to my death, I may bitterly weep for the offences that I have given Thee. I love Thee, O my Jesus: do Thou receive with kindness a sinner who wishes to love Thee. Recommend me, O Mary, to this Thy Son, who is in affliction and sadness for love of me.
I humbly pray: St. Alphonsus

Our Father

Again the second time, He went and prayed.
'My Father, if this chalice may not pass away,
but I must drink it, Thy will be done.'
Matt. 26:42
Hail Mary

When He returned, He found them again asleep,
for their eyes were heavy.
Mark 14:40
Hail Mary

He went again: and He prayed the third time,
saying the selfsame word.
Matt. 26:44
Hail Mary

'Sleep ye now and take your rest;
behold the hour is at hand, and the Son
of Man shall be betrayed into the hands of sinners.'
Matt. 26:45
Hail Mary

'Rise up, let us go.
Behold, he that will betray Me is at hand.'
Mark 14:42
Hail Mary

Cometh Judas Iscariot, one of the twelve:
and with him a great multitude with swords and staves.
Mark 14:43
Hail Mary

Coming to Jesus, he said: 'Hail Rabbi.'
And he kissed Him. 'Judas, dost thou
betray the Son of Man with a kiss?'
Matt 26:49 / *Luke* 22:48
Hail Mary

Jesus said to them: 'Whom seek ye?'
They answered Him: 'Jesus of Nazareth.'
John 18:4, 5
Hail Mary

'I am He;'
they went backward, and fell to the ground.
John 18:6
Hail Mary

Then they came up,
and laid hands on Jesus, and held Him.
Matt. 26:50
Hail Mary

Glory be to the Father.

O my Jesus, forgive us, save us from the
fire of hell. Lead all souls to Heaven,
especially those who are most in need.

Queen of the Holy Rosary,
be gracious to me and grant me the grace of

RESIGNATION TO THE WILL OF GOD

II
THE SCOURGING

$\mathfrak{M}$y beloved Saviour, I behold Thee all torn in pieces for me; no longer, therefore, can I doubt that Thou dost love me, and love me greatly, too. Every wound of Thine is a sure token on Thy part of Thy love, which with too much reason demands my love. Thou, O my Jesus, dost, without reserve, give me Thy blood; it is but just that I, without reserve, should give Thee all my heart. Do Thou, then, accept of it, and make it to be ever faithful.

St. Alphonsus

I humbly pray:

Our Father

Pilate said: 'But you have a custom
that I should release one unto you at the pasch:'
John 18:39
Hail Mary

'Whom will you that I release to you,
Barabbas, or Jesus that is called Christ?'
Matt. 27:17
Hail Mary

But the whole multitude together cried out, saying:
'Away with this Man, and release unto us Barabbas:'
Luke 23:18
Hail Mary

His wife sent to him saying:
'Have thou nothing to do with that just Man;
Matt. 27:19
Hail Mary

for I have suffered many things
this day in a dream because of Him.'
Matt. 27:19
Hail Mary

But they cried again, saying: 'Crucify Him, crucify Him.'
Luke 23:21
Hail Mary

'Why, what evil hath this Man done? I find no cause of
death in Him. I will chastise Him therefore, and let Him go.'
Luke 23:22
Hail Mary

'For I am ready for scourges:
and My sorrow is continually before Me.'
Psalm 37:18
Hail Mary

He shall be led as sheep to the slaughter,
and He shall not open His mouth.
Isaias 53:7
Hail Mary

And we have thought Him as it were a leper,
and as one struck by God and afflicted.
Isaias 53:4
Hail Mary

Glory be to the Father.

O my Jesus, forgive us, save us from the
fire of hell. Lead all souls to Heaven,
especially those who are most in need.

Queen of the Holy Rosary,
be gracious to me and grant me the grace of

PURITY

III
THE CROWNING WITH THORNS

This vile crowd, not content with having so barba-rously crowned Jesus Christ, wished to mock Him, and to multiply fresh insults and torments; and so they bent the knee before Him, and deridingly saluted Him, "Hail, King of the Jews;" they spat in His face, they struck Him with the palms of their hands; with cries and ridicule and contempt they vilely insult Him;

St. Alphonsus

I humbly pray:

Our Father

He will crown Thee with a crown of tribulation.
Isaias 22:18
Hail Mary

Soldiers began to salute Him: 'Hail king of the Jews.'
And they struck His head with a reed.
Mark 15:18, 19
Hail Mary

I have not turned away My face from them
that rebuke Me, and spit upon Me.
Isaias 50:6
Hail Mary

And Pilate saith to them, 'Ecce Homo!'
But they cried out: 'Away with Him;
away with Him; crucify Him.'
John 19:5, 15
Hail Mary

'Why, what evil has He done?'
But they kept crying out the more, 'Crucify Him.'
Mark 15:14
Hail Mary

Pilate saith; 'knowest Thou not that I have the power
to crucify Thee, and I have power to release Thee?'
John 19:10
Hail Mary

Jesus answered; 'Thou shouldst not have any power
against Me, unless it were given thee from above.'
John 19:11
Hail Mary

'Shall I crucify your king?'
The chief priests answered,
'We have no king but Caesar.'
John 19:15
Hail Mary

And Pilate taking water washed his hands
before the people, saying: 'I am innocent of
the blood of this just Man; look you to it.'
Matt. 27:24
Hail Mary

And the whole people answering, said:
'His blood be upon us and upon our children.'
Matt. 27:25
Hail Mary

Glory be to the Father.

O my Jesus, forgive us, save us from the
fire of hell. Lead all souls to Heaven,
especially those who are most in need.

Queen of the Holy Rosary,
be gracious to me and grant me the grace of

HUMILITY

IV
THE CARRYING OF THE CROSS

O my Redeemer! by the merits of this sorrowful journey of Thine, give me strength to bear my cross with patience. I accept of all the sufferings and contempts which Thou dost destine for me to undergo. Thou hast rendered them lovely and sweet by embracing them for love of us: give me strength to endure them with calmness. *St. Alphonsus*

I humbly pray:

Our Father

If any man will come after Me, let him deny himself,
and take up his cross, and follow Me.
Matt. 16:24
Hail Mary

And whosever doth not carry his cross
and come after Me, cannot be My disciple.
Luke 14:27
Hail Mary

Justice shall walk before Him:
and shall set His steps in the way.
Psalm 84:14
Hail Mary

And there followed Him a great multitude of people,
and of women, who bewailed and lamented Him.
Luke 23:27
Hail Mary

But Jesus turning to them said,
'Daughters of Jerusalem, weep not over Me;
but weep for yourselves and for your children.'
Luke 23:28
Hail Mary

'For behold, the days shall come, wherein
they will say: Blessed are the barren,
Luke 23:29
Hail Mary

and the wombs that have not borne,
and the paps that have not given suck.'
Luke 23:29
Hail Mary

'Then shall they begin to say to the mountains:
Fall upon us; and to the hills: cover us.'
Luke 23:30
Hail Mary

'For if in the green wood they do these things,
what shall be done in the dry?'
Luke 23:31
Hail Mary

And they bring Him into the place called Golgotha,
which being interpreted is, The place of Calvary.
Mark 15:22
Hail Mary

Glory be to the Father.

O my Jesus, forgive us, save us from the
fire of hell. Lead all souls to Heaven,
especially those who are most in need.

Queen of the Holy Rosary,
be gracious to me and grant me the grace of

PATIENCE IN ADVERSITY

V
THE CRUCIFIXION

O God! who shall not compassionate the Son of God, who for love of men is dying of grief on a cross? He is tormented externally in His body by the innumerable wounds, and internally He is so afflicted and sad that He seeks solace for His great sorrow from the Eternal Father; but His Father, in order to satisfy His divine justice, abandons Him, and leaves Him to die desolate and deprived of every consolation.

I humbly pray: St. Alphonsus

Our Father

They have dug My hands and feet.
They have numbered all My bones.
Psalm 21:7, 8
Hail Mary

Now from the sixth hour there was darkness
over the whole earth, until the ninth hour.
Matt. 27:45
Hail Mary

Jesus cried out with a loud voice, saying:
'Eli, Eli, lamma sabacthani?' That is,
'My God, My God, why hast Thou forsaken Me?'
Matt. 27:46
Hail Mary

My strength is dried up like a potshed, and My
tongue hath cleaved to My jaws. Jesus said: 'I thirst.'
Psalm 21:16 / *John* 19:28
Hail Mary

Putting a sponge full of vinegar about hyssop,
put it to His mouth.
John 19:29
Hail Mary

Jesus therefore, when He had taken the vinegar,
said: 'It is consummated.'
John 19:30
Hail Mary

And the sun was darkened, and behold the veil
of the temple was rent in two, and the earth quaked.
Luke 23:45 / *Matt.* 27:51
Hail Mary

And Jesus crying with a loud voice, said,
'Father, into Thy hands I commend My spirit.'
Luke 23:46
Hail Mary

And saying this, He gave up the ghost.
Luke 23:46
Hail Mary

Now the centurion, seeing what was done,
glorified God, saying: 'Indeed this was the Son of God.'
Luke 23:47 / *Matt* 27:54
Hail Mary

Glory be to the Father.

O my Jesus, forgive us, save us from the
fire of hell. Lead all souls to Heaven,
especially those who are most in need.

Queen of the Holy Rosary,
be gracious to me and grant me the grace of

LOVE OF OUR ENEMIES

Closing Prayers, page 84

$\mathcal{F}$ear not you; for I know that you seek Jesus who was crucified. He is not here, for He is risen, as He said. Come, and see the place where the Lord was laid.

Matt. 28:5, 6

THE GLORIOUS MYSTERIES

Prayer before the recitation:
In the name of the Father, and
of the Son, and of the
Holy Ghost.
Amen.

Then say:
Hail Mary.

IN THANKSGIVING

Your sorrow (says the Saviour, to encourage us) shall be turned into joy. Ah, my God, I deserve not Paradise, but hell; yet Thy death gives me a hope of obtaining it. I desire and ask Paradise of Thee, not so much in order to enjoy, as in order to love Thee everlastingly, secure that it will never more be possible for me to lose Thee.

O Lady, do Thou pray for me, for Thou wilt ask for the graces I require with greater devotion than I can dare to ask for them; and Thou wilt obtain far greater graces from God for me than I can presume to seek. St. Alphonsus

Queen of the Holy Rosary, I give Thee my heart in thanksgiving for this favor.

*Creed, Our Father, 3 Hail Marys,
Glory be to the Father.*

73

I
THE RESURRECTION

Jesus, Thou didst rise again the third day. I beseech Thee by Thy resurrection, make me rise glorious with Thee at the last day, to be always united with Thee in Heaven, to praise Thee and love Thee forever.
I humbly pray:

St. Alphonsus

Our Father

If Christ be not risen again,
then is our preaching vain, and your faith is also vain.
I Cor. 15:14
Hail Mary

Two of the disciples went to a town named Emmaus.
They talked together of all these things which had happened.
Luke 24:13, 14
Hail Mary

While they talked and reasoned with themselves,
Jesus Himself also drawing near, went with them.
Luke 24:15
Hail Mary

But their eyes were held,
that they should not know Him.
Luke 24:16
Hail Mary

'What are these discourses that you hold
one with another as you walk, and are sad?'
Luke 24:17
Hail Mary

They said: 'Concerning Jesus of Nazareth, Who
was a prophet. And how our chief priests delivered
Him to be condemned to death, and crucified Him.'
Luke 24:19, 20
Hail Mary

'Certain women also were at the sepulchre,
and not finding His body, also seen a
vision of angels, who say that He is alive.'
Luke 24:22, 23
Hail Mary

Beginning at Moses and all the prophets,
He expounded to them in all the scriptures,
the things that were concerning Him.
Luke 24:27
Hail Mary

And it came to pass whilst He was at the table with them,
He took bread, and blessed, and brake, and gave to them.
Luke 24:30
Hail Mary

And their eyes were opened, and they knew Him:
and He vanished out of their sight.
Luke 24:31
Hail Mary

Glory be to the Father.

O my Jesus, forgive us, save us from the
fire of hell. Lead all souls to Heaven,
especially those who are most in need.

Queen of the Holy Rosary,
be gracious to me and grant me the grace of

FAITH

II
THE ASCENSION

Ah, my God, make me love Thee exceedingly in this life, that I may love Thee exceedingly in eternity. Thou art the object most worthy of being loved; Thou dost deserve all my love: I will love none but Thee. Do Thou help me by Thy grace. I humbly pray: *St. Alphonsus*

Our Father

'You shall see the Son of Man sitting
on the right hand of the power of God,
and coming with the clouds of Heaven.'
Mark 14:62
Hail Mary

'And these signs shall follow them that believe:
In My name they shall cast out devils:
they shall speak with new tongues.'
Mark 16:17
Hail Mary

'They shall lay their hands upon the sick,
and they shall recover.'
Mark 16:18
Hail Mary

'For John indeed baptized with water, but you shall be
baptized with the Holy Ghost, not many days hence.'
Acts 1:5
Hail Mary

'Lord, wilt Thou at this time restore again the kingdom
to Israel?' But He said to them: 'It is not for you to know the
times or moments, which the Father hath put in His own power.
Acts 1:6, 7
Hail Mary

'You shall receive the power of the Holy Ghost coming upon
you, and you shall be witnesses unto Me in Jerusalem,
Acts 1:8
Hail Mary

and in all Judea, and Samaria,
and even to the uttermost part of the earth.'
Acts 1:8
Hail Mary

While they looked on, He was raised up:
and a cloud received Him out of their sight.
Acts 1:9
Hail Mary

Behold two men stood by them in white garments said:
'Ye men of Galilee, why stand you looking up to Heaven?'
Acts 1:10, 11
Hail Mary

'This Jesus who is taken up from you into Heaven,
shall so come, as you have seen Him going into Heaven.'
Acts 1:11
Hail Mary

Glory be to the Father.

O my Jesus, forgive us, save us from the
fire of hell. Lead all souls to Heaven,
especially those who are most in need.

Queen of the Holy Rosary,
be gracious to me and grant me the grace of

HOPE

III
THE DESCENT OF THE HOLY GHOST

Come, Holy Ghost, Sanctifier all powerful, God of love, Thou who didst fill the Virgin Mary with grace, Thou who didst wonderfully transform the hearts of the Apostles, Thou who didst endow all Thy martyrs with a miraculous heroism, come and sanctify us. Illumine our minds, strengthen our will, purify our consciences, rectify our judgments, set our hearts on fire, and preserve us from the misfortune of resisting Thine inspirations. Unknown

I humbly pray:

Our Father

And when the days of the Pentecost were accomplished, they were all together in one place:
Acts 2:1
Hail Mary

And suddenly there came a sound from Heaven, as of a mighty wind coming.
Acts 2:2
Hail Mary

And there appeared to them parted tongues as it were of fire, and it sat upon every one of them.
Acts 2:3
Hail Mary

And they were all filled
with the Holy Ghost,
Acts 2:4
Hail Mary

and they began to speak with divers tongues,
according as the Holy Ghost gave them to speak.
Acts 2:4
Hail Mary

Now there were dwelling at Jerusalem;
Jews, devout men, out of every nation under Heaven.
Acts 2:5
Hail Mary

And they were all amazed,
and wondered, saying: 'How have we heard,
every man our own tongue wherein we were born?'
Acts 2:7, 8
Hail Mary

But Peter, standing up with the eleven,
lifted up his voice and spoke to them.
Acts 2:14
Hail Mary

'Do penance, and be baptized; in the name of Jesus Christ
and you shall receive the gift of the Holy Ghost.'
Acts 2:38
Hail Mary

They therefore that received his word,
were baptized, and there were added
in that day about three thousand souls.
Acts 2:41
Hail Mary

Glory be to the Father.

O my Jesus, forgive us, save us from the
fire of hell. Lead all souls to Heaven,
especially those who are most in need.

Queen of the Holy Rosary,
be gracious to me and grant me the grace of

CHARITY

IV
THE ASSUMPTION OF OUR BLESSED
MOTHER INTO HEAVEN

Ⓞ Immaculate Virgin, Mother of God and Mother of men. We believe with all the fervor of our faith in Thy triumphal Assumption, both in body and soul, into Heaven, where Thou are acclaimed as Queen by all the choirs of angels and all the legions of saints; and we unite with them to praise and bless the Lord who has exalted Thee above all other pure creatures, and to offer Thee the tribute of our devotion and our love.

Pius XII

I humbly pray:

Our Father

Arise, make haste, My love, My dove,
My beautiful one, and come.
Cant. 2:10
Hail Mary

My soul doth magnify the Lord.
And My spirit hath rejoiced in God My Savior...
Luke 1:46, 47
Hail Mary

For behold from henceforth all generations
shall call Me blessed.
Luke 1:48
Hail Mary

Hearken, O Daughter, and see, and incline Thy ear:
and the King shall greatly desire Thy beauty.
Psalm 44:11, 12
Hail Mary

All the glory of the King's Daughter is within
golden borders, clothed round about with varieties.
Psalm 44:14, 15
Hail Mary

Who is She that cometh forth
as the morning rising, fair as the moon,
Cant. 6:9
Hail Mary

bright as the sun, terrible as an army set in array?
Cant. 6:9
Hail Mary

Thou art all fair, O My Love, and there is not a spot in Thee.
Cant. 4:7
Hail Mary

My heart hath uttered a good word:
I speak My works to the King.
Psalm 44:2
Hail Mary

Sing ye to the Lord a new canticle,
because He hath done wonderful things.
Psalm 97:1
Hail Mary

Glory be to the Father.

O my Jesus, forgive us, save us from the
fire of hell. Lead all souls to Heaven,
especially those who are most in need.

Queen of the Holy Rosary,
be gracious to me and grant me the grace of

UNION WITH CHRIST

V
THE CORONATION OF OUR BLESSED MOTHER IN HEAVEN AS ITS QUEEN

O great, exalted, and most glorious Lady, prostrate at the foot of Thy throne we adore Thee from this valley of tears. We rejoice at Thy immense glory, with which our Lord has enriched Thee; and now that Thou art enthroned as Queen of Heaven and earth, ah forget us not, Thy poor servants. Disdain not, from the high throne on which Thou reignest, to cast Thine eyes of mercy on us miserable creatures. The nearer Thou art to the source of graces, in the greater abundance canst Thou procure those graces for us.   St. Alphonsus
I humbly pray:

Our Father

And as the rainbow giving light in the bright clouds,
and as the flower of roses in the days of the spring...
Ecclus. 50:8
Hail Mary

In Me is all grace of the way and of the truth,
in Me is all hope of life and of virtue.
Ecclus. 24:25
Hail Mary

Come over to Me, all ye that desire Me,
and be filled with My fruits.
Ecclus. 24:26
Hail Mary

For My spirit is sweet above honey, and
My inheritance above honey and the honeycomb.
Ecclus. 24:27
Hail Mary

He that hearkeneth to Me,
shall not be confounded...
Ecclus 24:30
Hail Mary

She hath opened Her hand to the needy,
and stretched out Her hands to the poor.
Prov. 31:20
Hail Mary

Strength and beauty are Her clothing...
Prov. 31:25
Hail Mary

She hath opened Her mouth to wisdom,
and the law of clemency is on Her tongue.
Prov. 31:26
Hail Mary

Her children rose up, and called Her blessed...
Prov. 31:28
Hail Mary

Many daughters have gathered together riches:
Thou hast surpassed them all.
Prov. 31: 29
Hail Mary

Glory be to the Father.

O my Jesus, forgive us, save us from the
fire of hell. Lead all souls to Heaven,
especially those who are most in need.

Queen of the Holy Rosary,
be gracious to me and grant me the grace of

UNION WITH THEE

Closing Prayers, page 84

HAIL, HOLY QUEEN

Hail, Holy Queen, Mother of Mercy, Hail, our life, our sweetness, and our hope! To Thee do we cry, poor banished children of Eve, to Thee do we send up our sighs, mourning and weeping in this valley of tears. Turn then, Most gracious Advocate, Thine eyes of mercy toward us; and after this our exile show unto us the blessed Fruit of Thy womb, Jesus. O clement, O loving, O sweet Virgin Mary!

P. Pray for us, O Holy Mother of God.

R. That we may be made worthy of the promises of Christ.

TO OUR LADY OF HELP

Say not, merciful Virgin, that Thou cannot help me; for Thy beloved Son has given Thee all power in Heaven and on earth. Say not that Thou ought not to assist me, for Thou are the Mother of all the poor children of Adam, and mine in particular. Since then, merciful Virgin, Thou are my Mother and Thou are all powerful, what excuse can Thou offer if Thou do not lend Thy assistance? See, my Mother, see, Thou are obliged to grant me what I ask, and to yield to my entreaties.

Saint Francis of Sales

In Petition

Carry Thou, O Mary, our prayers within the sanctuary of the Heavenly audience, and bring forth from it the antidote of our reconciliation. May what we ask for with sure confidence, through Thee be granted. (*Specify request*). Hail Mary, etc.

St. Augustine

In Thanksgiving

I Venerate Thee, great Queen, and I thank Thee for the many graces Thou hast bestowed upon me even unto this day. (*Specify request*). Hail Mary, etc.

St. Alphonsus

PRAYER

O God! Whose only-begotten Son, by His life, death, and resurrection, has purchased for us the reward of eternal life; grant, we beseech Thee, that, meditating upon these mysteries of the Most Holy Rosary of the Blessed Virgin Mary, we may imitate what they contain and obtain what they promise. Through the same Christ our Lord. Amen.

V. May the divine assistance remain always with us.

R. Amen.

V. And may the souls of the faithful departed, through the mercy of God, rest in peace.

R. Amen.

In the name of the Father, and of the Son, and of the Holy Ghost. Amen.

Our Lady of the Blessed Sacrament, awaken in all believers a lively devotion toward the Most Holy Eucharist.

NOVENA RECORD

In Petition

1 J	2 S	3 G	4 J	5 S	6 G	7 J	8 S	9 G
10 J	11 S	12 G	13 J	14 S	15 G	16 J	17 S	18 G
19 J	20 S	21 G	22 J	23 S	24 G	25 J	26 S	27 G

In Thanksgiving

1 J	2 S	3 G	4 J	5 S	6 G	7 J	8 S	9 G
10 J	11 S	12 G	13 J	14 S	15 G	16 J	17 S	18 G
19 J	20 S	21 G	22 J	23 S	24 G	25 J	26 S	27 G

Use a regular calendar and write in the mysteries from the 1st to the 27th day in petition. Then on the 28th day, write in the mysteries to the 54th day for thanksgiving. As you complete each day, cross it off the calendar. This will better track your novena, as to which mystery you are on. If Sunday is the 1st day (Joyful) then on the second Sunday you would say the Sorrowful mystery.

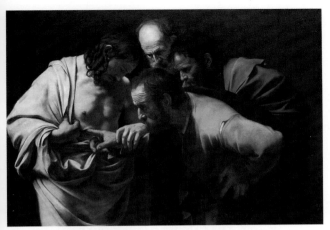

The doors were shut, and Jesus came and stood
in the midst, and said to them: 'Peace be to you.'

He shewed them His hands and His side. The disciples
therefore were glad, when they saw the Lord.

Now Thomas, one of the twelve,
was not with them when Jesus came.

The other disciples therefore said to him:
'We have seen the Lord.'

'Except I shall see in His hands the print of the nails,
and put my hand into His side, I will not believe.'

After eight days again, Jesus cometh and stood in
the midst, and said: 'Peace be to you.'

Then He saith to Thomas:
'Put in thy finger hither, and see My hands;'

'And bring hither thy hand, and put it into My side;
and be not faithless, but believing.'

Thomas answered, and said to Him:
'My Lord, and my God.'

'Because thou hast seen Me, Thomas, thou hast believed:
blessed are they that have not seen, and have believed.'

John 20:19 - 29

Fatima on July 13th, 1917₂

I shall come to ask for the consecration of Russia to My Immaculate Heart, and the Communion of Reparation on the First Saturdays. If My requests are heeded, Russia will be converted, and there will be peace; if not, she will spread her errors throughout the world, causing wars and persecutions of the Church. The good will be martyred, the Holy Father will have much to suffer, various nations will be annihilated. In the end, My Immaculate Heart will triumph. The Holy Father will consecrate Russia to Me, and she will be converted, and a period of peace will be granted to the world. In Portugal, the dogma of the Faith will always be preserved; etc... Do not tell this to anybody. Francisco, yes, you may tell him.

When you pray the Rosary, say after each mystery: O my Jesus, forgive us, save us from the fire of hell. Lead all souls to Heaven, especially those who are most in need.

THE FATIMA CRUSADER
Special Introductory Issue, Page 7.

Please pray that the Holy Father will consecrate Russia to the Immaculate Heart of Mary, in union with all the bishops.